A **R**ook**i**e reader®

Sir Mike

Written by Robyn Hood Black
Illustrated by David Murphy

Children's Press®
A Division of Scholastic Inc.
New York • Toronto • London • Auckland • Sydney
Mexico City • New Delhi • Hong Kong
Danbury, Connecticut

This book is dedicated to my noble son, Seth.
— R.H.B.

For my nephews Ethan, Jack, and Tommy.
— D.M.

Consultant
Eileen Robinson
Reading Specialist

Library of Congress Cataloging-in-Publication Data

Black, Robyn Hood, 1963–
  Sir mike / written by Robyn Hood Black ; illustrated by David Murphy.
      p. cm. — (A Rookie reader)
  Summary: Mike is all ready to fight the dragon he thinks he sees,
but then is happy to realize it is just his pet dog.
   ISBN 0-516-24862-6 (lib. bdg.)   0-516-25020-5 (pbk.)
  [1. Play—Fiction. 2. Dogs—Fiction. 3. Dragons—Fiction. 4. Stories in rhyme.]
I. Murphy, David, 1965– ill. II. Title. III. Series.
  PZ8.3.B57147Sir 2005
  [E]—dc22
                                2004030131

CHILDREN'S PRESS and A ROOKIE READER®, and associated logos are trademarks
and or registered trademarks of Scholastic Library Publishing. SCHOLASTIC and
associated logos are trademarks and or registered trademarks of Scholastic Inc.
1 2 3 4 5 6 7 8 9 10 R 14 13 12 11 10 09 08 07 06 05

I am Sir Mike.
I am a knight.

If I see a dragon,
I might have to fight.

There's a helmet on my head and sword in my hand.

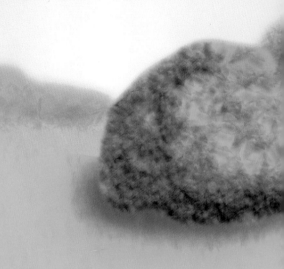

I have to go out.
This is my land.

Who's that over there?
Come into the light.

Did you hear me dragon?
Will you hide all night?

Look at my moves.
Are you ready for me?

I am so brave.
Come out here and see.

I can take on the tree
and strike at the swing.

I can hang upside down
and fight anything.

I can swing from the tree
and land over there.

I can charge from the slide
and fight anywhere.

I'm good with my sword.
I'm wild and I'm fast.

Once this battle starts,
I know it won't last.

Are you moving, dragon?
Will you attack?

The last dragon I fought
never came back.

Hurry up, dragon.
I'm ready to win.

You'll never come back
to my land again.

Wait! I know that nose.
I know those eyes.

You're not a dragon.

Woof! Woof! Surprise!

Word List (96 Words)
(Words in **bold** are story words that rhyme.)

a	**eyes**	in	on	those
again	**fast**	into	once	to
all	**fight**	is	out	tree
am	for	it	over	up
and	fought	**knight**	ready	upsid
anything	from	know	**see**	wait
anywhere	go	**land**	sir	who's
are	good	**last**	slide	wild
at	**hand**	**light**	so	will
attack	hang	look	starts	**win**
back	have	**me**	strike	with
battle	head	might	**surprise**	won't
brave	hear	Mike	**swing**	woof
came	helmet	moves	sword	you
can	here	moving	take	you'll
charge	hide	my	that	you're
come	hurry	never	the	
did	I	**night**	**there**	
down	if	nose	there's	
dragon	I'm	not	this	

About the Author

Robyn Hood Black lives in Gainesville, Georgia, with husband Jeff, dau ter Morgan, and son Seth. They share the realm with a variety of anim including horses, goats, dogs, and cats. Robyn's writing and artwork h appeared in newspapers and magazines. Her brave deeds have inclu teaching middle school English.

About the Illustrator

David Murphy is from Kansas City, Missouri. He has been drawing since was very small and would watch his grandmother paint. When he drawing or painting, David likes to visit the mountains to hike and ski.